IMAGES
of America
WINOOSKI

IMAGES
of America

WINOOSKI

Al Blondin and Anastasia Pratt
with the Winooski Historical Society

ARCADIA
PUBLISHING

Published by Arcadia Publishing
Charleston, South Carolina

Library of Congress Control Number: 2015936076

For all general information, please contact Arcadia Publishing:
Telephone 843-853-2070
Fax 843-853-0044
E-mail sales@arcadiapublishing.com
For customer service and orders:
Toll-Free 1-888-313-2665

Visit us on the Internet at www.arcadiapublishing.com

Dedicated to our families and to the people of Winooski

CONTENTS

ACKNOWLEDGMENTS

We are grateful to the many people who helped to make this project possible by contributing photographs and information. Included among them are Dan Higgins; Jim and Gloria (Cusson) Pratt; Peter and Judi DePaul; Dennis DePaul; Kelly DePaul; Richard Lyons; René and Peggy Cusson; Reginald and Jeannette Cusson; Diane Therriault Provost; Pauline Therriault Daggett; Mary Kinville; Sue Lavallee; Pamela Crosby; Doris Gamelin; Charles Thomas; Elaine Hancock; Ed McGuire and the Vermont French Canadian Genealogical Society; John Fisher; Roland Dion; *Look Around Winooski, VT;* the Chittenden County Historical Society; members of the "You know you grew up in Winooski because" Facebook group; and Christopher David Burns and the University of Vermont Special Collections Department.

We are also grateful to those Winooski residents who have so thoughtfully over the years preserved and turned over to the Winooski Historical Society so many photographs. We would also like to thank both past and present members of the Winooski Historical Society for the preservation of these photographs and artifacts and for allowing us to share them in this publication.

As in any collection of photographs, our choices were limited by access. We would love to include more families and businesses in future volumes. To help us do that, please consider sharing your photographs with the Winooski Historical Society.

Unless otherwise indicated, the photographs in this book come from the Winooski Historical Society.

INTRODUCTION

The city of Winooski, Vermont, located in the Champlain Valley and Chittenden County, was, in the beginning, a part of the town of Colchester. Governor Wentworth, also commander-in-chief of the province of New Hampshire, acting on behalf of King George III, granted the charter for Colchester on June 7, 1763. Edward Burling and 66 associates received the grant, which included the portion of Colchester that now comprises the city of Winooski. That charter, of course, ignored the fact that Native Americans had occupied the land for hundreds of years before European settlers arrived.

Ira Allen and his cousin Remember Baker surveyed the area later to be known both as Colchester and Winooski. They led a party of men to cut a road from Hubbardton north to the Onion River. Later, the same group of men would build a formidable blockhouse known as Fort Frederick along the Onion River for defensive purposes. This blockhouse would serve as a fort, a general store, and also home to the Onion River Land Company.

By 1783, Yankee farmers hungry for land began moving north, out of Massachusetts and Connecticut. Many settled in the region around Fort Frederick. Ira Allen was one of the people who decided to settle in this area. He built a house just north of Fort Frederick, facing the Onion River. Allen's construction of the house was the true beginning of growth in this area.

The waters of the Onion River and its falls provided an excellent source of power, allowing industries to start up. As well, the area around the falls of the Onion River provided a sustainable means of transportation to boats carrying supplies and building materials to a place now referred to as Allen's Settlement. Iron forges and lumber mills were located here, and roads heading north and east now led out of the area. Workers now began to settle, many migrating down from Canada. With their arrival, the portion of land around the river and falls eventually became known as the French Village.

In 1835, the first of several woolen mills was opened in the area. The shift toward industrialization sparked another rise in population, as many French, Irish, Polish, Italian, and Armenian families settled in the area to take up jobs in the mills. With the increased population came churches, businesses, and hospitals. The first church in Winooski, known as the First Congregational Church, was opened in 1840.

By 1866, the settlement around the river and falls, with its population of 1,745, would petition the Vermont Legislature to be known as Winooski Village. As the population grew, so did the need for education and churches. Accordingly, new churches and schools were built during the late 19th century. Also, other industries began to open up in the area, employing workers with a craft in wood products. During this era, many of Winooski's men served in the Civil War.

In the time from 1860 through 1872, Winooski would see the building of the Methodist and two Catholic churches in the area. In 1890, Winooski's desire to educate its children meant that the village featured a public school and a Catholic school at St. Francis Xavier. In addition, the village now included a general store and trolley service.

Throughout the 1900s, the area was to see much more industrial growth with the influx of textile mills. Houses of entertainment began to open their doors, welcoming audience members who worked in the local industries. As a result of those artistic developments, Winooski became an area rich in theater, music, and other cultural activities. At the same time, citizens recognized the importance of military service, with many enlisting during World War I.

Development of the Winooski's arts and culture occurred at about the same time that the village was changing politically. On March 22, 1922, by a vote of 176 to 78, the citizens of Winooski voted to ratify a 1921 Vermont State charter and the Village of Winooski became the City of Winooski. Measuring 795 acres, for a total of one square mile of land, the city officially separated from the Town of Colchester. At the same time, H.A. Bailey was elected the first mayor of Winooski, a fitting reward for having written the city's charter.

Unfortunately, soon after the incorporation, the flood of 1927 brought industry to a halt. Businesses and homes were washed away or destroyed, and the citizens of Winooski had to deal with this tragedy. Although the Great Depression, of course, affected the citizens of the city, by the mid-1930s, the downtown area saw continued growth, including through the creation of schools and churches.

Following World War II and the Korean conflict, both of which led to increased production for local mills, Winooski faced the loss of its primary industries. In 1954, the American Woolen Mill announced its intent to close its shops and move operations south, and the city was again devastated. Only one year before, the Porter Screen Company had closed its doors due to lagging sales and put 250 people out of work.

After these major setbacks, the city turned to the federal government, looking for grants to rebuild the city and to assist its citizens in finding new jobs. In 1967, Winooski was enrolled in the government's Model Cities Program. This program would allow the city to modernize its downtown area and encourage growth once again. This federal Model Cities Program would be closed down just as the area was being torn apart, leaving the city in a terrible position of losing a majority of its tax base.

In 1973, along with the failure of the Model Cities Program, Winooski suffered another setback in the loss, by fire, of the Vermont Furniture Company. This fire left another 250 people without jobs. Fortunately, in 1976, work began on the Highland Park section of Winooski, bringing new industries to the area.

Still later, around 1990, Winooski saw significant changes in the population and appearance of the city. The Refugee Resettlement Program chose Winooski as a resettlement site and, as a result, refugees from Sudan, Bosnia, and Vietnam came to and settled in the city. Also around this time, people began to talk about rebuilding the area that was devastated under the Model Cities Program. Just after the turn of the 21st century, plans were finalized and brought to the capital in Montpelier for approval and funding. By 2001, construction had begun. Done in phases, the construction was to include a new traffic roundabout to assist in keeping the traffic moving in the city.

Now, in 2015, Winooski includes new and old buildings and celebrates the customs and cultures of its varied residents. The downtown area includes restaurants, stores, and parks. Festivals and museums also bring people into Winooski.

One

WINOOSKI FALLS

In 1773, early settlers to the area built a block house. Fort Frederick was built of hewed timber and included 32 portholes. This marker was erected near the actual site of the fort by the Vermont Society of the Sons of the American Revolution in July 1914 to honor the work of Ira Allen, Remember Baker, and the other settlers who stood against "Indians and Yorkers."

The youngest brother of Ethan, Ira Allen was an early member of the Green Mountain Boys and one of the founding fathers of Vermont. He was one of the first settlers of Winooski Falls, and it was near there that Ira and his cousin Remember Baker established a structure that served as fort, house, and tavern.

Completed around 1840, this line drawing shows the lower falls of the Winooski River, a gristmill, and a covered bridge. In the distance, the First Congregational Church is visible. A covered waterway, to the left, carries water to the Burlington Woolen Mill, which is not shown. The Stone House is at the top of the drawing.

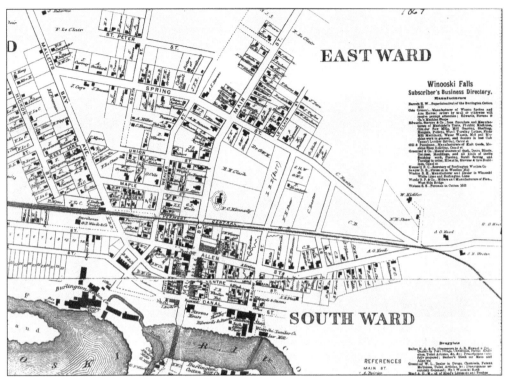

In 1869, Winooski Falls was divided into three wards: the West, the East, and the South Wards. Created from surveys completed by F.W. Beers, this map shows the eastern portion of Winooski, all of which lies north of the river.

The sawmill located on the Winooski side of the river at the upper falls is visible in this image. The Stone House can be seen in the background. This photograph was taken in 1900 from the Burlington side of the river.

Measuring 90 miles, the Winooski River is Vermont's longest and most important river. Useful for travel and for the water it brings to surrounding farmlands, the river has also given rise to various industries. Within the village and then city of Winooski, the river's two falls have long been used to produce power.

Winooski's main commercial area centers on Main and East Allen Streets. However, the residential areas of the village and then city were interspersed with businesses. This postcard, from the turn of the 20th century, shows the Winooski Block to the left and houses to the right.

12

In 1867, Francis LeClair, Charles Lafountain, and E.W. Chase hired Warren Thayer to develop plans for a three-story block to be built in the center of downtown Winooski village. The building was constructed by Frank Pepin and Peter Villemaire. All of the brick used in the building came from Francis LeClair's Mallets Bay Avenue brickyard, while the caps and sills for the windows were manufactured by the Edwards and Stevens foundry.

Built in 1900, the Brunswick Hotel was located on the corner of Main and East Canal Streets. Replacing the American Hotel, which was built in 1868 and was destroyed by fire in 1890, the Brunswick suffered foundation damage in the flood of 1927 and was later moved to a new location just a block away on East Canal Street. At that time, the hotel's name was changed, becoming first the Franklin Hotel and then the Deluxe Hotel.

Originally the site of Ira Allen's house and later the site of John Weaver's general store, the Winooski Block stands on the corner of Main and East Allen Streets. At various times, the block was home to establishments like the A&P Store, Richard's Drug Store, the George E. Allen Hardware store, the US Post Office, and the state-run liquor store. Even after revitalization efforts, the bottom floors of the block have continued to be a prominent commercial space. However, the third floor of the block contained a 60-by-53-foot concert hall in which both St. Francis Xavier and St. Stephen parishes celebrated Mass before their churches were built. The space was also used by musical groups, like Sherman's Cornet Band. The Sherman's Cornet Band was organized in 1871 by George D. Sherman and later became the Burlington Military Band, eventually moving to Burlington. Theatrical performances and other concerts also occurred within this very iconic building.

Prior to European settlement and as early as AD 750, Winooski Falls was occupied by members of the Abenaki tribe. The fertile river valley formed by the Winooski River and its waterfall made the land highly desirable, first as farmland and later as a means of power for the region's industry. After Ira and Ethan Allen settled the area in 1772, other European settlers arrived. Thought to be the second-oldest house in Winooski, this structure, known today as the Demers House, is located at 81 East Allen Street, next door to the Stone House. The house was built in 1827. First operated as an inn and tavern by James Hunter Platt, it was sold to Thaddeus Fletcher in 1847. In 1908, H.A. Bailey, the first mayor of Winooski, purchased the building, which is now owned by Rita Demers.

Located at 73 East Allen Street, the Stone House is the oldest house in Winooski. From 1793 until the early 1800s, this was the site of Brownell's Tavern, which included a rooming house. A place to exchange news and gossip, the Stone House was also the site of several early Colchester meetings. Once the home of the Winooski Historical Society, the house is a modified Georgian with a balanced facade. Made of sandstone, the house does not have floor joists. Rather, stone piers and walls in the cellar support the floor.

Corporation Hall was situated on the northwest corner of Main and West Center Streets. Constructed in 1878 by the Burlington Woolen Company, Inc., Carl Fehmer designed the building, and George Nash of Winooski constructed it at a cost of $8,500. The first floor housed the corporation store, from which mill employees were expected to purchase goods on credit against their wages. When Henry W. Mason, nephew of the mill's manager, ran off with the receipts, the store closed in scandal in 1881, after which the facility was rented to Safford, Humphrey, and Company, a dry goods store that was the first facility in Winooski to adopt electricity. The hall was also used for social events. In 1915, according to *Fibre and Fabric*, the hall was used for socials that included music "furnished in the evening by an Italian orchestra and in the afternoon the Sherman Band."

Members of the Winooski Water Department stand on the banks of the Gill Brook, an early source of water that lies northeast of the city. Pictured are, from left to right, unidentified; John Kelty, mayor; Maurice Paquette; William Allen; and Arthur Barron.

Fire Alarm Boxes

3	Station Call	3
5	Factory Outlet Store	5
6	Porter Screen Co.	6
7	Main and East Allen Streets	7
8	River and Forrest Streets	8
12	Barlow and East Center Streets	12
13	East Allen and East Streets	13
14	West Canal and Morgan Streets	14
15	West Allen and Malletts Bay Avenue	15
23	Leclair and Spring Streets	23
24	Fire Station Main Street	24
25	Franklin and Lafountain Streets	25
26	East Allen and Manseau Streets	26
27	Upper Heights	27
31	River and Hickok Streets	31
32	Elm and West Streets	32
33	Spring and Malletts Bay Avenue	33
34	Weaver and Spring Streets	34
35	St. Peter and North Streets	35
36	Malletts Bay Avenue and Pine Streets	36
37	Hall and Audette Streets	37
41	Union and North Streets	41
42	Main and Lafountain Streets	42
43	Main and Bellevue Streets	43
44	Lafountain and Whitney Streets	44
45	East Allen and Roland Court	45
51	Main and West Canal Streets	51
61	St. Michael's College	61
62	Fanny Allen Hospital	62

Winooski Police Dept. Tel. UN 4-4470

Winooski Fire Dept. Tel. UN 3-3321

HOSPITALS: Mary Fletcher Tel. 4-7441
Fanny Allen Tel. 4-4501
DeGoesbriand Tel. 3-3451

The Winooski Fire Department, for many years, relied on citizens to raise the alarm when a fire was spotted. This list shows the locations for all of the fire alarm boxes located throughout the city in 1869. Although both St. Michael's College and the Fanny Allen Hospital are located in Colchester, they were part of the Winooski Fire District.

Two

FAMILY LIFE

John and Anna (Fortuna) DePaul sit with their children, John Jr., Peter, and Jeannie. The DePauls married on June 24, 1936, at St. Stephen's Church. John spoke both English and Italian fluently while Anna added French to the mix. Together, they raised a family and owned and operated a shoe store in Winooski. Anna also served as Dr. Louis Thabault's first nurse. (Courtesy of Peter and Judi DePaul and of Dennis DePaul.)

Mary Augustino's wedding party poses together on August 6, 1955. The daughter of Salvatore "Sam" and Rosaria (Fazzateli) Augustino married Louis Lawrence, son of Louis and Josephine (Pidgeon) Lawrence. From left to right are Anna Augustino, Fran Augustino, Mary Augustino, Arlene Plant Augustino, June Gibson Lee, and Donna Dattilio (in the front). The photograph on the wall shows the bride's parents and their oldest daughter, Catherine (Augustino) Dattilio. (Courtesy of Gloria Cusson Pratt.)

Sister Marie of the Assumption, born Robertine Bourassa, celebrates her 70th birthday in this photograph. Born to Alphonse and Vitaline (Leblanc) Bourassa in 1902, Sister Marie ultimately spent 74 years in active and devoted religious service with the Sisters of Providence. (Courtesy of John Fisher.)

In 2005, members of the Winooski Historical Society celebrated Dorothea Cameron's 100th birthday at Starr Farm Nursing Home. Cameron taught at the Memorial School for many years. A parishioner of St. Stephen's Parish, she served as the congregation's organist for 63 years, retiring on August 9, 1984. From left to right are (first row) Florence Saucier, Dorothea Cameron, and Josephine Galle; (second row) Sheila Blondin, Helen Braddock, Jean DeVarney, Mary Ellen Fitzgerald, Dick Lesage, and Julie and Bill Crenshaw; (third row) unidentified, Tom Devine, and Rita Martel.

Wilfred Lapointe poses with his new bride, Bertha Lapointe. The couple married at St. Francis Xavier Church on September 16, 1924. Bertha grew up on West Street. Her husband was the son of Edward and Marie Louise (Langlois) Lapointe. Among other things, Wilfred worked at General Electric and sold summer cottages in Malletts Bay. (Courtesy of Gloria Cusson Pratt.)

Joseph and Harriet (Sidney) Blondin, captured in this family photograph, were members of the Winooski community in the late 1800s and early 1900s. Joseph served in the Civil War in the Vermont Regiment Company I. Joseph Blondin also served his community for three years as a village trustee. (Courtesy of Alfred Blondin.)

The family of Alphonse and Leona (Leclair) Bourassa appears in this image. In 1912, Alphonse, who had been missing for four months, was discovered off Colchester Point. Reports suggested that he had fallen from the bridge while crossing to Burlington. Leona was left with eight children to support. (Courtesy of John Fisher.)

The Dion family is pictured. They are, from left to right, (sitting) Wilfrid Dion, father; Germaine Dion Smith; Corrine Dion, mother; and Cecile Dion L'Ecuyer; (standing) Juliette Dion Leblanc, Antonio Dion, Henri Dion, Philip Dion, Annette Dion, and Gerard Dion. The Dion family lived on a 100-acre farm at 291 East Allen Street. Through the years, they provided lots on Dion Street to their family members for the construction of homes. New streets in the area were named after their children, Gail, Bernard, Roger, and Reginald.

The Cusson family lived on West Street in Winooski, in a house that Ephreme built by connecting two smaller structures. Shown here are, from left to right, (first row) Ephreme, Armand, Bertha, Albina, Adelard, and Anastasie; (second row) Rose, Marie, and Beatrice. Six generations of the Cusson family have lived and continue to live in Winooski. (Courtesy of Gloria Cusson Pratt.)

The Dufresne family was photographed in 1949. Sisters Cecile Dufresne Messier, Theresa Dufresne (Sr. Mary Regis of the Sisters of Providence), and Marie-Anne Dufresne Bergeron stand behind their father, Regis, founder of the Dufresne Filling Station (1937) and Dufresne's Fuels (1947); mother Dorilda (Couture) Dufresne; and brother Paul Dufresne.

On September 1, 1962, at St. Francis Xavier Church, Leon John Provost, son of Allen Edward and Orrena Theresa (Cavanaugh) Provost, married Diane Louise Therriault, born May 31, 1942, to Henry and Celina (Valley) Therriault. The Provosts had four sons. (Courtesy of Diane Provost.)

24

Marcel and Theresa (Therriault) Cote grew up in Winooski and settled there after their marriage on July 5, 1958. Marcel and his brother Roger, who married sisters, were two of Omer and Eleanore (Marcotte) Cote's 10 children, all of whom grew up on Weaver Street. (Courtesy of Diane Provost.)

A Winooski elementary school teacher for 50 years, Irene McGettrick attended a 1946 summer session at the University of Vermont. She was born on June 12, 1896, to Louis N. and Catherine Hardacre Devino, married Edward B. McGettrick, and died in August 1983. McGettrick is buried in St. Joseph Cemetery in Burlington.

John and Yvonne (Provost) O'Brien are shown in this photograph. When the couple married, Yvonne could only speak French, while John could only speak English. They later had three sons, Tom, Robert, and William. John O'Brien was manager of the American Woolen Mill.

Mary Rose Delage, daughter of Edward and Theresa (Charpentier) Delage, married Henry Girard Therriault, son of Henry and Eva (Bousquet) Therriault, on January 6, 1951, at St. Francis Xavier Church. The couple raised 10 children in Winooski. Subsequently, some of those children raised their families in the city. (Courtesy of Pauline Therriault Daggett.)

Horace Luther Thomas was born in 1846 to Robert Clifford and Agnes McWhirter, Irish immigrants who lived in Winooski. A self-taught electrical engineer, Thomas ran the hydroelectric power plan on the Winooski River. In 1896, he was involved in an industrial accident at the power plant when he was caught in an electric dynamo. (Courtesy of Charles Thomas.)

Anna Clifford, born on August 2, 1851, was the wife of Horace Thomas and the mother of three daughters and two sons. In her obituary, her family described her as "a woman of retiring disposition, always devoted to her family and friends." (Courtesy of Charles Thomas.)

Ray Preavy served in France during World War II. When he was in the United States, he also served as the bass player for Don Field's Pony Boys Band, which broadcast from WDEV in Waterbury during the 1930s and 1940s. (Courtesy of Pamela Crosby.)

Nick Parrino photographed Pfc. Leonard L. Sweeney of Winooski in 1943. Sweeney, who worked as a mechanic in his civilian life, was a truck driver in the US Army. The photograph was taken as part of the Office of War Information's Overseas Picture Division.

The Thabault family served Winooski for years as doctors. George, the father (left), was joined in the medical profession by sons Louis (right) and Wilfred. Wilfred's obituary stated, "Following in the steps of his father, and oldest brother Dr. Louis Thabault, he pursued a career in medicine and a devotion to the French community of Winooski."

Clement and Edna Parsons were the first Winooski family to sell their home to the Urban Renewal Agency, after which they moved to Platt Street. Parsons was a volunteer fireman who worked at the Woolen Mill and later at the Porter Screen Factory. He was known for always being available to help people. (Courtesy Richard Lyons.)

Dan Higgins's photograph shows the Lulic family, who resettled in Winooski after leaving Bosnia. Since 1989, more than 6,300 refugees have resettled in Chittenden County. Now Winooski's citizens claim various ethnic heritages. They are, to mention a few groups, French Canadian, Irish, Italian, Polish, Bosnian, Tibetan, Vietnamese, and African. (Courtesy of Dan Higgins.)

Simon, Atem, Chol, Deng, and Panther are seen in a photograph from Dan Higgins's book *Vacancy, Art & Transformation*. The men in this image relocated to Winooski after their journey through Africa. Part of a group known as the Boys of Sudan, they are seen here posing with an onion—a symbol of their new hometown—in their hands. (Courtesy of Dan Higgins.)

Three

RELIGION

St. Stephen Parish was founded in 1870, when the Reverend Thomas Lynch organized a congregation that used the concert hall in the Winooski Block for its services. In 1871, the congregation purchased a parcel of land on Barlow Street. The new church, whose cornerstone was blessed by the Bishop Louis deGoesbriand, officially opened in the spring of 1872.

Despite the construction of the church in 1871 and 1872, St. Stephen Parish was a mission of the Catholic cathedral parish in Burlington until 1881. At that time, the Reverend John S. Michaud was appointed the first resident pastor of the parish, and in 1882, the rectory was built. Reverend Michaud served in this capacity until the fall of 1885. During his tenure, he made various improvements to the parish.

On April 16, 1928, construction of a new and larger St. Stephen's Church began. The marble church offered its first Mass on Christmas Eve of the same year and was dedicated on September 29, 1929. The old church, in the background, was moved back to make way for the new structure, which was built from marble shipped by rail from Proctor, Vermont. While the new church was being built, parishioners attended Mass in the old church.

The elaborate wood carvings within St. Stephen's Church were created by Albert H. Whittekind, a parishioner who lived on East Allen Street. Whittekind carved the priest's bench, credence table, and baptismal font cover, along with hundreds of other items during his nearly 75-year career. The parish also boasts a marble statue of Our Sorrowful Mother, which was erected in 1949 to commemorate Winooski citizens who died during the First and Second World Wars.

This photograph offers a vision of the altar in the marble church built for St. Stephen Church. From 1928, this altar has graced the church. It is possible that Whittekind, who carved several components of the first altar, did some of the side carvings for the new building.

Msgr. John B. McGarry served as pastor of St. Stephen Parish, doing all of the jobs normally undertaken by a parish priest, from 1915 until his death in December 1951. Monsignor McGarry was instrumental in organizing and raising funds for the new marble church in 1928. As parish priest, he performed all of the sacraments, including marrying couples.

Men from St. Stephen Parish stand beside Msgr. John B. McGarry (center, first row). The other men are, from left to right, (first row) Ralph Aruzza, Michael Deady, Monsignor McGarry, James Smith, and Tom Fitzgerald; (second row) Lester Cruse, a Mr. Parreau, and John O'Brien; (third row) Father Carrigan (behind column), Robert Bashand, Edward Dorey, and Francis Corrigan.

In 1939, the St. Stephen's choir included, among others, Geneva Devino, Frederic Blais, Albert Gravel, Betty Horton Yates, Rachel Germain, Shirley Hughes, Theresa St. Peter, Jane Horton Blondin, Marguerite Blair, Cecile Blais, Ellen Germain, Louis Abair, and Irene St. Peter.

St. Francis Xavier Church was established after Bishop Louis deGoesbriand conducted a survey of Winooski and discovered more than 800 French-speaking Roman Catholics in the village. Rev. Jean Audet was the parish's first priest, arriving more than two years before the church was constructed and opened in December 1870.

Reverend Audet, a native of Quebec, continued to serve the parish for 49 years. Funding for the church that was built after his arrival came from pledges and donations, all offered at the great personal sacrifice of the parishioners. One parishioner in particular, Francis LeClair, sold the church 10 acres of land—enough for the church, rectory, and cemetery—for $4,000 and then continued to direct the construction while furnishing the bricks and wood needed at a much reduced price. Later, in 1882, the parishioners mounted a fundraising campaign to build steeples and purchase a carillon. At one point, St. Francis Xavier Church offered Masses at 5:00 p.m. and 7:00 p.m. on Saturday and at 7:00 a.m., 8:30 a.m., 10:00 a.m., 11:30 a.m., and 7:00 p.m. on Sunday. The parish also built a dual French-English school to serve parishioners; the school offered classes through the eighth grade.

Adelard Cusson, son of Ephreme and Anastasie, was born and raised in Winooski. A devout Catholic, he was confirmed in the faith at St. Francis Xavier Church and continued to attend the parish for the rest of his life. (Courtesy of René and Peggy Cusson.)

Adelard and Rita Cusson's oldest daughter, Gloria, stands beside a white picket fence on her First Communion day. Like many French Canadian families in Winooski, the Cussons were active members of St. Francis Xavier Church. In fact, five generations of the family have called the parish home. (Courtesy of Gloria Cusson Pratt.)

La Société des Enfants de Marie participated in this early-1940s May Crowing at St. Francis Xavier Church. Included in the image are Jeanne Dion, Jeannine Bourassa, Cecile Rocheleau, Russell Parizo, Bernadette Leclair, Rita Feeney, Raymond Frenette, Susan Valley, Aline Thibault, Yvonne Thibault, Agnes Hebert, Lucille Thabault, Marie-Jeanne Paquette, Fr. Edward Gelineau, Alice Leblanc, Emelda Lacharite, Alice Lesage, Rita Vallee, Lorraine Rocheleau, Lorraine Debarge, Theresa Potvin, Laurette Lesage, Margaret Duval, Doris Bissonnette, Lillian Lesage, Beatrice Duhamel, Cecile Beauchemin, Pauline Sourmail, Yvette Duhamel, and Rita Boisjoli.

Sodality members of St. Francis Xavier Church who participated in the May Crowning ceremony in 1937 included Claire Villemaire, Bernard Couture, Raymond Brault, Rev. Wilfred Gelineau, Rita Lesage, Gertrude Granger, Jeanne d'Arc Lamothe, Jeannette Mongeon, Yvonne Guerin, Jeanne Brault, Rev. George L'Ecuyer, Agnes Hebert, Anita De Varney, Mignonne Godin, Berthe Bissonnette, Therese Hebert, Evelina Lacharite, Seraphine Chastenay, Blanche Lord, Noella Lamothe, Edna St. Pierre, Germaine Bigue, Blanche Langlais, and Ethel Stuart.

Robertine Bourassa graduated from the St. Louis Convent School in 1918 and later went on to become a nun in the order of the Sisters of Providence. This photograph captures the celebration of her 50th anniversary within that order. On her death, she was remembered as a woman of faith, devotion, and prayer. (Courtesy of John Fisher.)

The Methodist church was built in 1860 at a cost of $3,000. On Sunday December 16, 1917, the church burned down and was rebuilt in December of the following year. During the winter of 1899, the Methodist church offered a 10:00 a.m. service for the Mizpah Brotherhood and a 10:30 a.m. regular service with sermon. Sunday school was convened at noon, with a teacher's meeting at 6:00 p.m. and the Epworth League prayer meeting at 7:00 p.m.

Rebuilt in 1928, the Methodist church is located on the corner of Follett and West Allen Streets. In 1922, the church acquired a bell from the defunct First Congregational Church. Being interested in the social lives of its members, who included soldiers from the nearby Fort Ethan Allen, the church included a lecture room and social room in the new structure. Although the wooden Methodist church remains modest in appearance, it has served the community well.

Trinity Episcopal Mission Church on Platt Street was designed by the Reverend John Henry Hopkins Jr. It was consecrated on July 5, 1877, by the Right Reverend Bishop Bissell, of the Vermont Diocese. Designed in the Gothic style, the church is made of wood with vertical batten sides. The open, ribbed roof and ceiling show alternate strips of black ash and pine. A screen of black ash divides the nave from the chancel. Two stained-glass windows—one designed by the Reverend John Henry Hopkins—allow light to stream into the church.

Four

EDUCATION

The Spring Street Schoolhouse was built in 1864 to meet the educational needs of the children of the Winooski Falls and Colchester areas. The growing industry in and around Winooski Falls brought more families to the area, and the community recognized the importance of early education for its children. The St. Louis Convent School quickly followed.

By 1890, the need was great enough for the town fathers to add a large addition to the present Spring Street School. Enrollment had about doubled with the addition of the high school grades. In 1890, Winooski-Colchester saw its first high school graduation. Winooski saw more graduates each year, until the school closed in 1912. A much larger brick high school was built on the site for the start of the 1913 school year.

While the commencement exercises were occurring at Corporation Hall in June 1912, construction workers were busy cutting this school in two and moving the pieces across the street. By September, the new brick building was open for students, and the old schoolhouse, moved across the street, was being converted into apartment houses.

The Winooski High School class of 1912 included Elsie F. Fiske, Thomas B. Fitzgerald, and Joseph W. Allard. Also shown here is the school's principal, George R. Stackpole. These were the last students to graduate from the original high school on Spring Street.

This is the new brick high school that replaced Spring Street School in 1912. Located on the same site, the high school served the needs of the community through 1959, when a larger and more modern structure was built on Upper Main Street.

Memorial School opened in September 1930. Situated on the corner of Union and North Streets, the school included 12 classrooms and administrative offices, as well as the only gymnasium in the city. Once students completed the eighth grade here, they would move on to Winooski High School. The school closed in the 1980s.

In 1939, eight classrooms were added to Memorial School. With that addition, the school was able to accommodate more of Winooski's students. As a result, Elm Street School closed and Memorial School's enrollment increased to 800 students. It is now an apartment building.

In 2007, members of the Winooski High School class of 1957 came together for a three-day reunion event. This banner was displayed on the fence that surrounds the "new" Winooski High School. The class of 1957 is known as one of the more active classes. Although there were only 40 graduates that year, most of them still live in Winooski or the surrounding areas.

The members of the class of 1957 in attendance at the 50th reunion were, from left to right, (first row) Beverly (Myers) Villemaire, Joan (Mercure) Danis, Joyce (Venezia) Tasetano, Carol (Perrotte) Hamner, Janet (Gamelin) Duncan, Carleen (Kirby) Ward, Rita (Companion) Weston, Alfred Blondin, Joan (Barcomb) Blondin, Dolores (Valdez) Huff, and Richard Soucy; (second row) James Ticehurst, George Bouffard, Earl Jones, James Weston, Faye (Paquette) Parr, Ronald Muir, Frank Chupka, and Edgar Sabourin. (Courtesy of Alfred Blondin.)

Members of the men's choir from the Winooski High School class of 1957 sing their theme song, "The Class of '57 Had Their Dreams." Pictured are, from left to right, James Weston, James Ticehurst, Ron Muir, George Bouffard, and Al Blondin. (Courtesy of Alfred Blondin.)

Women from the Winooski High School class of 1957 girls' choir entertain their classmates at the 50th reunion anniversary of their graduation. They are, from left to right, Carol (Perrotte) Hamner, Beverly (Myers) Villemaire, Rita (Companion) Weston, Joyce (Venezia) Tasetano, and Carleen (Kirby) Ward. (Courtesy of Alfred Blondin.)

Taken at the entrance of the Winooski High School on East Spring Street, this photograph shows the Winooski High School Chorus in 1946–1947. Among them are Theresa St. Peter, Fay Labelle, Theresa Sansoucy, Catherine Vartuli, Theresa Laferriere, Cecile Sauve, June Beaudoin, Gertrude Fournier, Darlene Dorey, Mary Ann Dufresne, Joy Companion, Charlotte Villemaire Theresa Lefebvre, Mary Merchant, Frances Prior (accompanist), Shirley Paquette, Jeannette Boucher, Ellen Germain, Barbara Arcand, Jeannete Bunnell, Leonard Barron, Donald Companion, Carl Provost, Paul Hardy, Ernest Vuley, Peter Handy, Theodore Companion, Lafayette Saucier (the director), Leon Ignazewski, Leo Villemaire, Lawrence Handy, Herman Poulin, George Lacharite, and Thomas Sullivan.

Kindergartners from St. Francis Xavier School are shown at their graduation. The tuition-based school offered classes in both French and English, alternating between the two languages spoken by the families of the parish. After the eighth grade, students wishing to continue with their education were then registered at Winooski High School, and those wishing to continue their Catholic education were registered at Mount St. Mary's or Rice High schools. (Courtesy of Gloria Cusson Pratt.)

The 1967 graduation exercise for Winooski High School was held on June 18 at the Winooski High School auditorium. Fifteen different awards were presented during the ceremony, and the guest speaker was J. Warren McLure, publisher of the *Burlington Free Press*. There were 102 graduates in the class.

Huard Studios, a photography studio in Winooski, captured this image of St. Louis Convent School graduates in June 1918. The convent was located on West Spring Street. Included are Aurore Brault, Robertine Bourassa, Prosper Frenette, Joseph Provost, Fréderic Blais, Lorenzo Germain, and Léonard Hatin.

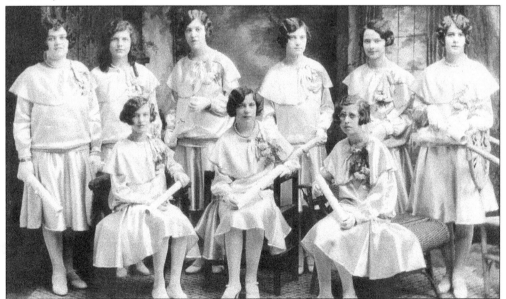

Claire Picher, Pauline Desaultels, Alice Lesage, Florence Nasby, Marguerite Yandow, Cécile Boissy, Florence Poirier, Anna Mae Desautels, and Gertrude Granger constituted the St. Louis Convent School class of 1929. They are shown here in a photograph taken by Huard Studios.

By 1944, the St. Louis Convent School was coeducational. The class of 1944 included George Lacharité, Bernard Lefebvre, Bernard Parent, Jean Côté, Roger Chicoine, Robert Thibault, Carl Provost, Edmond Soutière, Theresa Leblanc, Claire Bellefeuille, Lucille Ferland, Mae Marcotte, Jeannette Beauchemin, Claire Jarvis, Jeannine Lacharité, Thérèse Therrien, Béatrice Frégeau, Claire Hatin, Theresa L'Ecuyer, Laurette Lesage, Claire Duprat, Joyce Lebeau, Theresa Thabault Marie-Rose Delage, Armand Sénésac, Eugene Gaboury, Roland Rochette, Robert "Amos" Matte, Eugene Brunelle, Paul Leclair, David Gauthier, Paul Dufresne, Norman Bouffard, Leona Lebeau, Paul Lefebvre, Edmont St-Jacques, and Jeannette Boucher.

Members of the 1954 eighth grade graduation class at St. Francis Xavier included Jackie Frenette, Patricia Poulin, Yvonne Thibault, Barbara Standwick, Joan Daigle, Pauline Lesage, Lucille LaCroix, Rita Feeney, Arline Brunnelle, Margaret Johnson, Claire Audette, Anne Marie Decarreau, Carol Thibault, Gloria Dufresne, Pauline Barsalou, Jeanine Bourassa, Claire Limoges, Russell Pariseau, Sue Valley, Aline Thibault, Dale and Darlene Boucher, Albertine Lefebvre, Jackie LaPierre, Bernadette LeClerc, Edmund Berteau, Ray Frenette, Norman Audette, Robert Racicot, Lee Bourdeau, and Roger Derby. (Courtesy of Mary Kinville and Sue Lavallee.)

Graduates of St. Louis Convent, Winooski, Vermont, are pictured here in June 1939. From left to right are (first row) Y. Roy, H. Debarge, R. Villemaire, A. Bourdeau, C. Crowley, S. Brunelle, R. Bouchard, and A. Leblanc; (second row) A. Mongeon, A. Manseau, and A. Cote; (third row) R. Soutiere and A. Campbell; (fourth row) R. Bissonnette, O. Lamothe, R. Corbiere, R. Benoit (Benway), and C. Bergeron; (fifth row) S. Perrotte, A. Meunier, L. Robert, and G. Thabault; (sixth row) E. Lacharite and A. Cote; (seventh row) B. Duprat, L. Lefebvre, A. Sansoucy, G. Provost, and R. Villemaire; (eighth row) G. Whittle, E. Paquette, D. Barron, B. Lesage, G. Contois, L. Granger, and T. Boucher.

The 1956 St. Francis Xavier eighth grade class suffered an incredible loss on August 21, 1960, when seven of their classmates died in a tragic car accident. William Landino and Maurice Soutiere (seen among their classmates here), along with Norman Paquette, James Daigle, Edward Foley, Earl Decarreau, and Ronald Rogers, all lost their lives when their car careened out of control on US 2, north of the causeway in South Hero. (Courtesy of Gloria Cusson Pratt.)

One division of the St. Francis Xavier eighth grade class stands at the main entrance of the church in June 1961. Included in the photograph are Aline Brousseau, Diane Marquis, Susan Bulin, Elizabeth Villemaire, Rachel Piché, Rosemary Barber, Ernest Lavigne, Robert Frenette, Raymond Brunelle, Thomas Landry, Janet Deforge, Linda Meunier, Linda Bissonnette, Sandra St-Jacques, Susan Meunier, Claude Piché, Michael Simard, Irène Leclerc, Doris Gamelin, Gibby Sénésac, Raymond Meunier, Patrick Dion, Robert Marcotte, Maurice Roy, Roland Viens, and Edward Lacroix.

Sr. Georgette Rochon's eighth grade class, standing in the school gym in June 1976, included JoAnn Brodeur, Marie Grenier, Deborah Lovejoy, Carla Coolidge, Mary Ann Gaboriault, Peter Crowley, Robin Critchlow, Kathy McCormick, Colleen Frémeau, Rachel Plourde, Marc Viens, Jeffery Piché, Alfred Key, Gérard Bouffard, Stephen Roy, Gérard Thibault, Sean Gregorek, Patrick O'Connor, Michael Reardon, Jérome Bourgeois, Scott Lacourse, and James Robert.

Memorial School utilized a school patrol. Members of the patrol manned street corners, helping their schoolmates to cross safely. It was an honor to be chosen to serve. Members of the school patrol took their task very seriously and were rewarded at the end of the school year by a statewide outing. This 1977 group includes Rita Gendron.

The officers of Winooski's Future Teachers of America from the 1962–1963 academic year sit on the school's stage with the principal, Donald A. Brown (third from left). The students are, from left to right, Doris Gamelin, Judy Allen, John Hatcher, Peter DePaul, and Richard Desautels.

Members of the Winooski community were photographed while attending one of the many historical presentations given by members of the Winooski Historical Society. Among the topics covered over the years are Winooski Falls, the city of Winooski, the various businesses within the city, and the school system.

The Winooski Historical Society was established in 1975 with a mission of preserving and celebrating the history of Winooski. Originally located in the Stone House, the museum moved to the Champlain Mill in 2005. The museum was at first situated on the ground floor, but thanks to the generosity of the owners, it has since moved to street level, occupying a prime spot that overlooks the downtown area.

Among the items on display at the Winooski Historical Society Museum are photographs of the city and its residents, furniture hand carved in Winooski, a replica of St. Francis Xavier Church created with Popsicle sticks and glue, and signs from local businesses.

Citizens of Winooski gather to learn more about their history in 2010. They sit in the Champlain Mill, outside of the Winooski Historical Society Museum. The mill, renovated in 1981 to provide office and commercial space, was further renovated in the early part of the 21st century.

Five

BUSINESS AND INDUSTRY

The Porter Screen Company, whose wagon is shown here, expanded during the 1900s and started making ironing boards, pastry boards, chairs, and other wooden products. A fire in 1923 and the flood in 1927 hurt the company, though it was the decline in demand for wooden screen doors that caused the shop to close in 1952.

The Porter Screen Company began in Burlington in 1885, when E.N. Porter invented a successful door bracket. Around 1893, the company relocated to Winooski. After a fire, a new office was built at Spring Street. Farrell Distributing Corporation took over the buildings in 1959, using it as storage and warehouse space. Later, the US Department of Housing and Urban Development converted the buildings into the Courtyard Senior Housing, which opened in 1981.

The original home of Richard Manufacturing on Union Street appears in this image. The business was started by Eugene and Omer Richard in the backyard of a property owned by Eugene. It featured a line of cabinets, desks, screen doors, and caskets. Seen in this photograph are Omer Richard, Eugene Richard, Simeon Brosseau, Joseph Fortin, Jules Lord, Arthur Alarie, and Joseph Laferriere, along with several of the first employees at the Richard's factory.

As the demand for their product increased, the Richard brothers sought out land on Malletts Bay Avenue, in the area of the railroad depot, to build and expand their business. This image shows the company's second location in 1919. An expansion project was undertaken in 1927, making the factory considerably larger than when it opened.

This photograph shows the Vermont Furniture Company, formerly known as Richard Manufacturing Plant, located on Malletts Bay Avenue, near the railroad track. On July 24, 1973, the factory burned to the ground. Some 250 to 300 employees found themselves out of a job after the fire, although the company did continue to work in alternative locations.

Gale Lefebvre explains that she started working at Vermont Furniture, once known as Richard Manufacturing, as soon as she graduated from high school in 1965. She says, I "worked for them even after the fire. We moved the offices to Porter Screen the day after the fire and then the offices moved to Colchester for a few years. Vermont Furniture contracted with a New Hampshire company to make their furniture."

Lewis Wickes Hine visited Winooski in September 1910. In his capacity as an investigative photographer for the National Child Labor Committee, Hine travelled around the country photographing children at work. He noted 27 children apparently under the age of 15 at the American Woolen Mill.

A 1921 publication produced by the American Woolen Company indicates that the two mills—known as the Burlington Mills and the Champlain Mills—produced kerseys, friezes, meltons, thibets, worsted dress goods, piece-dyed worsteds, and serges. These boys were all employed, in some capacity, at the mills.

Taken at lunchtime in the drawing-in room of the American Woolen Company, this Lewis Hine photograph as taken May 5, 1909. In the group are the following: Alexina Lavalley, Anna Cross, Cecile Cauchon, Lena Campbell, and Albina Seymour. Hine noted that he counted 20 girls under the age of 14 going into the mill at 7:00 a.m.

Tessie McGrath, Sadio Finnegan, and Bernice Bedard—two of whom, Hine wrote, looked to be under 14—are seen at their noon hour. The girls stood in the drawing-in room, which was used to pull ends of fiber together. The machines that did that work could draw in 70 ends per minute.

Albert Lavallee was 14 years old when Lewis Hine photographed him in Winooski. Beginning work at the American Woolen Company, Lavallee was illiterate. Children were frequently sent to work in the mills so that they could contribute to their family's livelihood.

Although not identified by name, this group of boys worked at the American Woolen Mills in Winooski. The youngest boy in the photograph was 13 years old, and the oldest was 15. Hine identified most of the boys as illiterate. The lack of education received by children sent to work in factories was a primary concern of the National Child Labor Committee.

This girl, headed to work at the mill, was not identified by name in Hine's photograph. However, she is fairly typical of the girls who were employed in mills throughout New England. Girls and boys were particularly valuable within factories because their smaller size allowed them to fit in places adults could not.

All of the images of young mill workers featured here were part of Lewis Hine's photographic essay titled "Child Labor in Burlington and Winooski." Hine was dedicated to providing full captions, working in a series, and rigorously controlling the relationships within individual images.

Not all of the American Woolen Company's employees lived in Winooski. Young mill workers and older mill workers travelled from the surrounding communities, including Colchester and Burlington, to earn their paychecks doing the various tasks required by the mill.

Many of the families who called Winooski home relied on the mills for their livelihood. Parents and children often toiled side by side in the factories, all contributing to the family's income. These American Woolen Mill workers are primarily young, illustrating the lack of child labor laws in the United States. In fact, although child labor laws were proposed, passed, and repealed earlier, the first laws that truly regulated child labor were passed after the Great Depression.

Though these two young girls look like they are on their way to school, they are actually walking toward the mills. In June 1851, the *Burlington Free Press* ran a serialized novel by T.S. Arthur. Titled *The Factory Girl*, the novel portrayed the life of a farm girl forced to go to work in the mills of Lowell, Massachusetts, when her family fell on hard times. That story served as an inspiration to girls throughout Burlington and Winooski.

In this 1954 photograph, textile Workers Union of America members line up outside of the American Federation of Labor and Congress of Industrial Organizations (AFL-CIO) headquarters on Main Street in Winooski. They were present to vote on conditions for a strike against the American Woolen Mill. Union headquarters was situated near Epstein's, a grocery store.

Pictured above in 1929 is Arthur A. Bouffard, a route delivery man for the H.J. Mercure Creamery at 36 East Allen Street.

This photograph of the Porter Screen and Warehouse and Distributing Company, Warehouse No. 11, on East Spring Street, was taken as part of the Historic American Buildings Survey. Sanders Milens took the picture, while Emily J. Harris served as the project's historian.

The American Woolen Company on East Canal Street was photographed as part of the Historic American Engineering Record. Jean P. Yarby and Monica E. Hawley worked on the project, which focused—at least in part—on brick buildings and on the textile industry.

Bruce Clouette served as the historian on the Historic American Engineering Record project for which the Burlington Woolen Mill Company and Dam were photographed. Although it sits west of the bridge on the Burlington side of the river, this mill was one of the industries centered on the Winooski River and employing Winooski's residents.

Beginning in 1869, the Baxter Block (to the right) was the site of an elementary school run by the Sisters of Charity of Providence. Designed for the children of French-speaking Catholic families, the school enrolled 80 students its first year with each of those students paying 20¢ a month for tuition. On January 7, 1869, the sisters, who had been living in Burlington, moved to Winooski and opened the St. Louis Convent School on West Spring Street. When a traveling preacher was available and while they were raising script to build their own church on the plot of land donated to them, the Methodists used the hall in the Baxter Block for services.

The Star Bakery at 7 West Canal Street was owned by John Trono, father of Mike Trono and stepfather to Frank Perrino. Seen here are, from left to right, Joseph Mazza Sr., George Pepin, John Trono Sr., and Frank Perrino. The bakery served the city, selling cookies and donuts to mill employees on their way to and from work. Just about every Friday, the Star Bakery sold out of fresh bread dough, which was a staple for the numerous Catholic families living in the city.

Maternities, Inc., a sewing company, employed a variety of Winooski citizens, including Jane Rabidoux, Marie Pepin, Thelma LaRocque, Rose Allen Monahan Risik, Hazel Savage Mason, Esterleen Fortin Dion, and Jean Young Brown. Here, employees from the company are on a family outing in 1952. By the mid-1950s, the factory was known as Essex Manufacturing, which—under the management of Mr. and Mrs. Alfred Ticehurst (both in the photograph)—specialized in children's clothing. The building on Center Street is now home to Dan Higgins Photo Studio.

From 1918 until 1926, the A&P Store, managed by James A. Bruce, was located on Main Street. Among the items offered for sale in the store were canned and dry goods, fruits, teas, coffee, and other supplies for the house. The A&P was far from the only store in Winooski. Others included McBride's Meat Market, Parizo's Groceries, Melnick and Epstein Market, Mercure's Creamery, Landry's IGA, Germain's Store, Tom's Market, Seymour's Store, Boucher's Store, and Chick's Market.

In 1932, Wasilkowski's Dry Goods and Tobacco shop, located on 11 West Canal Street, was photographed with Tony Wasilkowski and Victoria Bonk standing ready to serve customers. Later stores in the area included the Grand Union, the IGA, Forest Hills Factory Outlet, and Merle Wood's Country Store.

The Clavelle brothers' IGA was located on West Allen Street and managed by brothers Robert and Raymond Clavelle. Among the goods offered for sale at this store were assorted crackers; sugar, flour, and other baking supplies; soda; baby food; and toilet paper and other paper products. They also did a big business in fresh-cut meats. Clavelle's IGA opened in 1948 and closed in 1959, unable to compete with the larger supermarkets moving into the area.

The A.J. Lesage Market was situated at 93 West Street. This 1950 photograph shows, from left to right, Ernest, Francis, Alice, Claire, mother Clara, father Alfred Lesage, Roger, Leonard, Conrad, Clement (at the wheel of his Model T), Maurice, and Romeo. (Courtesy of University of Vermont Special Collections.)

One of Dan Higgins's photographs for *Vacancy, Art & Transformation*, this image shows a woman calling Bingo at the Corporation Hall. Bingo has long been a staple of Winooski's social life, with sessions held on behalf of the St. Francis Xavier Church and the senior citizens' center. (Courtesy of Dan Higgins.)

The Green Mountain Lunch, a restaurant at 22 Main Street, is shown here on February 3, 1949. Owned and operated by Samuel and Olida Moroian, the restaurant was located in a building that belonged to Ralph Bernadini. Originally, the restaurant was known as the Green Mountain Lunch and Ice Cream Parlor.

Sulham's Sweet Shop, located at 60 Main Street, offered holiday cheer to its customers in 1945. Harold Sulham, behind the Coca-Cola machine, and his wife, Evelyn, a waitress behind the bar, owned the shop. Also included in the photograph are Jimmy Morwood, Fred Maynard, Johnny Provost, Charles Crowley, Francis Mongeon, Charlene Sullivan, and Theresa Ledoux. In this photograph, the restaurant owners and customers were ringing in the new year. Throughout the city, as well as throughout the country, festivities to celebrate the turning of the year were customary, with parties, concerts, and other revelries. The photograph also calls to mind the family nature of many of Winooski's businesses, which were often owned and operated by married couples, by successive generations of a family, or by siblings.

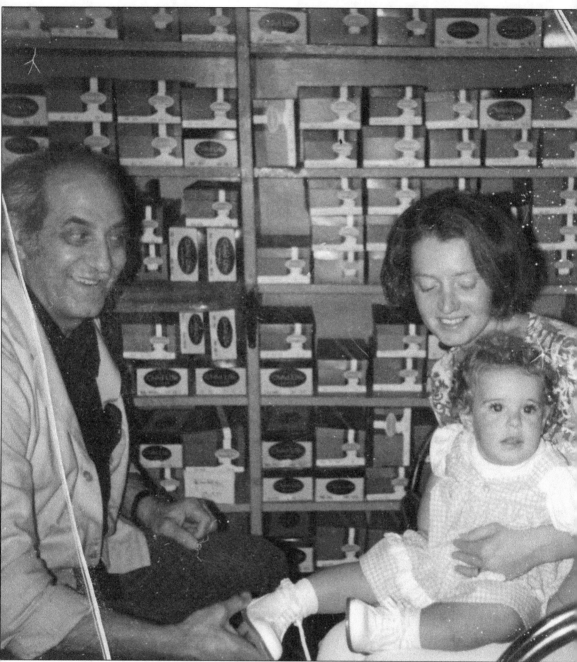

John DePaul started selling Child Life shoes after he completed an apprenticeship in Keeseville, New York. During his repairs of the company's shoes, he decided that he liked the quality of the product. The DePauls were noted for telling parents that they should not buy shoes for their children before the old pair was worn out or before they were old enough to walk. In turn, customers were loyal to the store, whose owners they could trust. The DePauls were caring in other ways, too. John often "gave away" his repair work and with his wife, Anna, loaded their car with the shoes they could not sell and brought them to St. Joseph's Orphanage so that the children could have new shoes. (Courtesy of Judy and Peter DePaul.)

Located on Main Street, Sneaker's Bar and Grill—now Sneaker's Bistro—has long been known for its high-quality food and, during the 1980s, for its jazz and bluegrass shows. Marc and Jean Dysinger currently own the restaurant, which opened in 1980 with house specialties of eggs Benedict, Belgian waffles, pancakes, and French toast. (Courtesy of Gloria Cusson Pratt.)

In 1952, Louis L. McAllister photographed the staff of the Ernest Lesage Fuel Service, which was situated at 104 Malletts Bay Avenue. From left to right, the staff members are Ernest Lesage, Norman Ducharme, Gerald Pepin, Joye Companion Dorcy, Jerome Martel, Leonard Lesage, and Albert Mongeon. (Courtesy of the University of Vermont Special Collections.)

Bernie Gervais's Barbershop, which moved to West Canal Street in 1985, was the site of many haircuts. Above, one fourth-generation Winooski citizen, Mark Cusson, received his first haircut on April 23, 1982; below, his brother Rene received his first haircut on February 23, 1985. Both brothers went on to graduate from the Winooski High School, each taking an active role in the school's athletic program. (Courtesy of René and Peggy Cusson.)

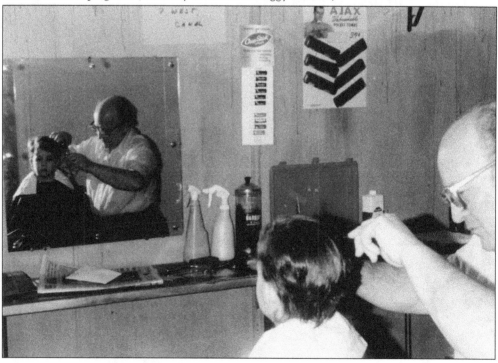

Six

FUN AND RECREATION

Standing from left to right, Douglas Cauchon, Bradley Mayo, and Wesley Carroll watch George Bouffard (left) and Albert Quinton (right) play chess at the Teenage Club. The Teenage Club was located in the upper floor of the city hall building, situated on the corner of West Allen and Weaver Streets. This building was once the home of the First Congregational Church.

From left to right, Maurice Germain and Richard Prairie play cribbage at the Teenage Club. The Teenage Club provided much after school and evening entertainment for the youth of Winooski. Raymond Villemaire and Charles Crowley actively supervised and oversaw the entire operation, which included a wide range of activities.

Among the activities sponsored by the Teenage Club were weekend dances, like this one from 1955. Local bands would play at some of the dances, while records would be spun for others. A special dance—the King and Queen Ball—was also held each year.

The Winooski Shuffleboard League was very active during the 1970s. This photograph, which comes from Dan Higgins's book *Vacancy, Art & Transformation*, shows several members of the league in 1977. Local restaurants—like Bernadini's and Bond's—sponsored teams, as did other organizations. (Courtesy of Dan Higgins.)

From left to right, Blanche Lord, Theresa LaMothe, Maurice Paquette, Alice Sansoucy, Madeleine Picher, and Agnes Hebert are seen during a theatrical performance. Winooski has hosted several theater groups, local and visiting, throughout its history. That dramatic tradition has continued through the high school, which regularly participates in local drama festivals.

One of the very active theater groups in Winooski posed for this photograph. This group performed in the upper hall of the Corporation Block, located at the corner of Main and West Center Streets, during the 1930s, when there were three or four theater companies.

In 1945, the Winooski High School baseball team included, from left to right, (first row) Babe Potvin, Alan Billups, Doe Thompson, Ray Villemaire, Bob Blanchard, Don Companion, and Tom Sullivan; (second row) John Provost, Earl Brunelle, Gerard Villemaire, Gerry Green, coach Pro Herbert, Ron Benway, Don Leduc, and Howard Vuley.

The 1949 St. Stephen's baseball team included Sherm Gilbert, Howard "Doe" Thompson, Doug Crowley, Bob Bouffard, Alan Provost, John Provost, and Don Leduc. Baseball has long been popular in Winooski, with teams fielded by the local schools, churches, and social organizations.

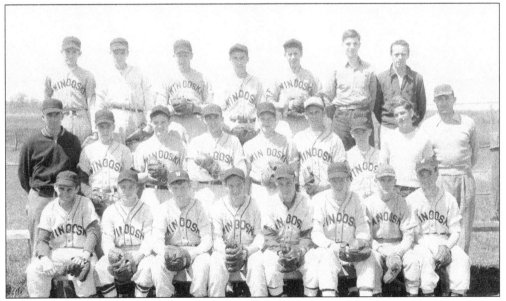

The 1951 Winooski High School baseball team featured Alan Provost, Doug Cauchon, Norm Fregeau, Joe Myers, Gerald Francis, Bob Gamelin, Ray Chicoine, Brad Mayo, Pro Herbert, Bob Landry, Wesley Carroll, Bob Gauthier, Roy Despirito, Alan Francis, Dave Lister, Tom Muir, Stan Yankowski, Joe Bourassa, Paul Boissy, Lou Provost, Earl Kirby, Ed Audette, George Gamelin, and Bob Bouffard.

Winooski's baseball team from 1951 featured Dick Poulin, Lee Paquette, Gil Barney, Doug Cauchon, Alan Provost, Norm Fregeau, Bob Gamelin, Bob Gauthier, Bob Bouffard, Don Lefebvre, Brad Mayo, John Crowley, Joe Myers, Pete Lacourse, Bob Decarreau, Ed Audette, Bob Landry, Guy Devarney, Neil Perrotte, Ray Chicoine, Earl Kirby, and coach Pro Herbert.

The 1929–1930 Winooski High School women's basketball team included, from left to right, (first row) Van Galaise (right guard), Betty Sprout (left forward), Jerry Mongeon (right forward), Helena Mayo (center), and Frances Sullivan (left guard); (second row) Elizabeth Lavallee (forward), Julie Desautels (forward), coach Scott Welch, and Gertrude Mongeon (guard).

The 1938 men's baseball team was photographed on the side entrance at Memorial School after a very successful season. Pictured are, from left to right, (first row) Clement Carroll, Ralph Lapointe, Norman Bean, Pete Houle, and Robert Merchant; (second row) Tony Scichitano, George Burke, Henry Guerin, and Calvin Parrow; (third row) Coach Lanahan, Stedman Huard, Chick Merchant, Jimmy Madison, and Francis Lacroix.

The 1911–1912 Winooski High School basketball team included Roscoe Little, Bob Hardacre, Joe Finnegan, Lawrence Hanley, Buster Potvin, and J.B. Fitzgerald. George R. Stackpole served as the team's coach. Stackpole supervised the school district and also served on the board of trade.

The 1952–1953 Winooski High School basketball team, led by Pro Herbert, included team members David Lister, Bob Landry, Lee Paquette, Gerald Francis, Alan Francis, Joe Bourassa, Bob Decarreau, Ron Myers, Dick Bouffard, Charlie Seymour, Roger Curran, Leon Sabourin, Paul Boissy, Paul Couture, Ernie Rochefort, Don Brunelle, Wesley Carroll, and Ted Beaudoin.

Longtime coach and principal John "Pro" Herbert demonstrates a ball-handling technique for the 1953–1954 Winooski High School men's basketball team. Watching intently are Dick Bouffard, Paul Boissy, Larry Allard, Dave Lister, Leon Sabourin, Joe Bourassa, and Bob Landry.

In 1945, Babe Potvin, Tom Sullivan, Bern L'Ecuyer, Jim Fitzgerald, Don Companion, Bill Skerneski, Ray Villemaire, Don Leduc, Howard Thompson, Chuck Abair, Norm Poulin, Hank Bouffard, Gerald Zeno, Ron Benway, Francis Mongeon, John Bedrosian, Ted Companion, Peter Mattos, Gene Brunelle, Ernest Vuley, Armand Niquette, Leslie Reid, and Gerard Villemaire played basketball for Winooski High School under coach Pro Herbert.

Winooski's basketball team won the state championship in 1949. Included on the team were Norm Bergeron, Bill Arcand, Paul Lister, Dick Sweeney, Gerry Green, Bob Bouffard, Don Lacharité, Marcel Fregeau, Jim Myers, coach Pro Herbert, Paul Kane, Dick Langlais, Gerald Seymour, and Doug Crowley.

Coach Pro Herbert worked with the 1949 basketball team that included Norm Bergeron, Paul Lister, Paul Kane, Gerry Green, Dick Sweeney, Marcel Fregeau, Dick Langlais, Gerald Seymour, Joe Caforio, Don Lacharité, Bill Arcand, Bob Bouffard, Carl Racine, Jim Myers, and Doug Crowley..

Butch Lapointe, Ken Atkins, Ray Frenette, Ray Rochefort, Paul Fortin, Rod Fitch, Walt Campbell, Gerald Sweeney, Paul Niquette, Bill Germain, and Bert Villemaire comprised the 1957–1958 Winooski High School men's basketball team. Coach Pro Herbert stands in the second row, center.

The Winooski High School women's basketball team members of 1946–1947 are, from left to right, Joan (Kane) Kirby, Gloria Parizo, Shirley (Paquette) Villemaire, Lorraine (Granger) Corbierr, Audrey (Mayo) Leduc, Katherine (Vartuli) Scott, Norma (Millette) Larrivee, June (Beaudoin), and Theresa Sansoucy.

The Red Wings were considered by the *Burlington Free Press* to be a "famed old Winooski team which made its mark in New England and Canadian hockey rinks." Playing during the late 1930s and early 1940s, the team used a rink on St. Peter Street, west of St. Francis Xavier Church. The parish school now occupies the site. From left to right are (first row) R. Poirier, R. Louiselle, and R. Frenette; (second row) E. Provost, unidentified, R. Lesage, B. Poirier, T. Bissonette, and P. Lesage.

Two members of the Winooski Red Wings hockey team, Romeo Louiselle (left) and Leo Bissonette (right), stand on the ice, while spectators watch from the edge of the rink. In the background, St. Francis Xavier Church is visible. While the team members were well padded, they did not wear helmets.

The 1944–1945 St. George Club Hockey team poses for a picture. Father St. Onge, from St. Francis Xavier Church, organized the St. George Club, which offered activities for parishioners. The brick house located at Pine and North Streets was especially popular because of the ice rink, which was used for hockey.

Football has been a staple of Winooski High School since 1931, with generations of family members playing for the Spartans. This varsity game, from 1997, included players like Mark Cusson, Jeremy Ravelin, Jim Marrier, Tom Cota, Mike Hemingway, Rob Hemingway, and Matt Maskell. (Courtesy of René and Peggy Cusson.)

Winooski High School has also featured several impressive soccer teams. This junior varsity team, from 1999, included Andrew Mumford, Andrew Viens, James Viens, René Cusson II, Matthew Hamilton, and Ted Dion, as well as several students from Bosnia. A very popular sport in Europe, soccer did not become common in the United States until the 20th century. Winooski sponsors soccer teams through the junior and senior high school and also through a youth soccer league for students beginning in kindergarten and ending in fifth grade. (Courtesy of René and Peggy Cusson.)

Seven

CIVIC ORGANIZATIONS

Beginning in the second half of the 19th century, Winooski's residents founded several volunteer fire departments. The Winooski Engine Company (also known as the Steamer Company) and the Sawyer Hose Company (later the Lafayette Fire Company) were both active, with the latter often serving as an Irish social club.

Located on Main Street from 1927 until it burned down in 1977, the firehouse is fondly remembered in Winooski. The alarm sounded every day to signal 5:00 p.m. and also utilized coded whistles to alert firemen as to the location of the emergency. Throughout the city, residents heard the alarms and responded.

After a 1977 fire destroyed the Winooski Firehouse, a new building was erected on the opposite side of Main Street, next door to the Lavigne Funeral Home. Rescued from the rubble, the firehouse bell was moved to the front lawn of the local Veterans of Foreign Wars post on the corner of Main and Maple Streets. This photograph was taken by Dan Higgins as part of the *Great Onion* book. (Courtesy of Dan Higgins.)

Taken on the steps of the old Winooski City Hall, at the northwest corner of Weaver and West Allen Streets in 1932, this photograph shows the Ste-Thérese Drill Team of Conseil J.F. Audet of L'Union St-Jean-Baptiste d'Amérique. Pictured are, from left to right, (first row) Laurette Poirier (Jasmin), the captain; (second row) Ida-Mae St-Pierre (Dion), Agnès Lamothe, Edna St-Pierre (Hatin), Marie-Marthe Rocheleau (Cole), Simonne Morin (Lavallée), and Desneiges Barsalou (Garcia); (third row) Anita Carrière (Atkins), Rita Bouffard (Vartuli), Françoise Bleau (Tremblay), Lucille Babeu (Andrew), Helene Jasmin (Baillargeon), Florence Dupuis (Allard), Anita Mongeon (Quill), and Beatrice Jasmin (Barre); (fourth row) Alice Mongeon (Frenette) and Yolande Rocheleau (Rousselle).

Parishioners of St. Francis Xavier Church were quite proud of their French Canadian heritage, forming a council of the Societé St. Jean Baptiste D'Amérique. The society's purpose was to "unite in a true spirit of brotherhood all persons of French origin residing in the United States, promote their individual and collective betterment and provide relief to its members and their beneficiaries."

Members of the 50th Anniversary Celebration Committee of Winooski posed for this photograph. From left to right are (first row) Mayor Dominique Casavant; (second row) Louis-Guy Rocheleau, Edmund Villemaire, Richard Lesage, Clement Bissonette, Austin Gloyd, and Clement Parsons; (third row) Edmond Villemaire, George Bechard, Roland Frenette, David Muir, and Fr. Philip Boisvert; (fourth row) James Myers (at far left, standing sideways), Dr. John Fitzgerald, Andre Bouchard, and Charles Villemaire.

The 1944 Knights of Columbus Mustache Club included Frank Perrino, Leo Decarreau, Theodore Perrotte, John Hammond, and Arthur "Shuffy" Tamer. The group sponsored a dance at the city hall. Among the patriotic decorations and to the music of Bob Mario and his orchestra from Burlington, the 10 members of the group appeared for the last time with their Lenten moustaches.

Members of the 1947 Mustache Club of the Knights of Columbus included Frank Perrino, Leo Decarreau, Albert Bissonette, John Hammond, Leon Germain, Arthur "Shuffy" Tamer, Fred "Turk" Laferriere, Romeo Loiselle, Theodore Perrotte, J. William O'Brien, Paul Marcotte, Wilfrid Thabault, and Raymond Decarreau.

A Catholic fraternal organization, the Knights of Columbus was founded in 1882 by Fr. Michael McGivney, in New Haven, Connecticut. The group's purpose was to serve the church, community, and family with virtue. The 1955–1956 officers of the Knights of Columbus of St. Stephen's Church included Edward Huard, Maurice Paquette, Frank Perrino, Leo Lefebvre, Russell Niquette, Frank Patenaude, James O'Hagan, William O'Brien, Leo Decarreau, Reginald Desautels, Pepper Martin, George Leduc, Paul Crowley Sr., and William Hebert.

The Knights of Columbus Mustache Club received their mustache cup award at the Lincoln Inn Banquet room in this 1948 photograph. It was the custom for members to grow a mustache during the Lenten period, after which a banquet was held and an award given for the best mustache. Members of the club included Harvey Meunier, Paul Crowley, Turk Laferriere, Antonio Scichitano, Paul Marcotte, Shuffy Tamer, Gerald Goyette, Raymond Decarreau, Donald Barron, Frank Perrino, John Hammond, Romeo Loiselle, Felix Bissonnette, Bernard Brown, Albert Gay, Leon Germain, Harold Brisson, Edward Devino, Albert Bissonnette, and James Shea.

Thirty years after its organization, the Conseil St. Laurent No. 35 of the Societe St. Jean Baptiste D'Amerique bought the Corporation Block in June 1931. A mutual benefit society, the Conseil St. Laurent was joined in 1921 by Conseil J.F. Audet No. 377, a women's council. At that point, the society numbered 500. This photograph was taken in 1903 in front of the St. Francis Xavier rectory. Father Audet—with the white beard—appears in the center of the photograph. St. Jean Baptiste is particularly important to French Canadians and to Franco-Americans, as the celebration of his birth on June 24 is a national holiday in Quebec. On that day, French Canadians and French Americans celebrate their heritage, their language, and their religion.

Officers from the Ethan Allen Post No. 32 of the American Legion in Winooski are shown on March 6, 1942, purchasing a $1,000 Defense Bond. From left to right are district commander Isaac Potvin; sergeant at arms James Carroll; superintendent of the Winooski Post Office Fred Pine; senior vice commander Harry H. Pratt; service officer and steward Hubert P. Gadue; post commander Severin Beaudoin, who is being handing the bond by Fred Pine; chaplain and past commander Arthur L. Mongeon; and finance officer Joseph Savard.

The charter members of the Madonna Circle of the Daughters of Isabella (1946) are, from left to right, (first row) F. Cauchon, A. Thibault, A. Manning (state regent), L. Adams, M.E. Fitzgerald, D. Poplawski, and H. Parizo; (second row) R. Smith, B. Devino, A. Picard, L. Sheppard, Father Fitzsimmons (state chaplain), H. O'Hagan, R. Germain, and D. Trono; (third row) L. Ducharme, P. Perrote, G. Devino, R. Roy, R. Farrell, and A. Meunier.

Members of the Winooski Historical Society stand inside the Stone House holding signs to remember various aspects of Vermont and Winooski history. From left to right are (seated/kneeling) Paul Richard and Rita Martel; (standing) Florence Saucier, Raymond Roy, Alice Meunier, Mary Ellen Fitzgerald, Jeannine Picher, and Dr. John Fitzgerald. One sign remembers Russell Niquette, a Winooski lawyer; another recalls Winooski residents who died in foreign wars.

Rita Martel, known for her outstanding work in the community, stands beside Vincent Edward Feeney, author of *The Great Falls on Onion River: A History of Winooski, Vermont*, during a book-signing event. Feeney's book tracks the community from its original settlers through 2002. Also included in the work are accounts of the creation of the City of Winooski.

This celebration included Paul Gunther Jr., Paul Gunther Sr., John E. O'Brien, Harvey Martin, Frank Patenaude, Bob Roy, Willie Goodreau, Pepper Martin, Henry Merchant, Tom McCormick, Larry Yandow, and Clem Parsons. The men had gathered at the old firehouse to celebrate the chief's birthday.

A group of Modern Woodmen of America stands at attention. The nationwide organization, beyond providing insurance and financial services, strives to honor relationships by acting with honesty, integrity, and respect; to be good stewards; to honor families, communities, and country; and to be accountable as individuals and as an organization.

Edna Lyons Parsons, married to Clement Parsons and mother of two daughters, Marie and Frances, was an artist and musician. Her last song, "The Winooski Firemen's March," heralds the volunteer firemen who "stand tall among the men who save our country, prepared to give your all." (Courtesy of Richard Lyons.)

The Winooski Cub Scouts Pack No. 658, seen here in 1993, included several leaders. Shown here are some of the leaders, John Sneck, Steve Ploesser, Dustin Bushway, Michael Bryant, Brother Roger (the St. Francis Xavier Parish representative), and René Cusson. (Courtesy of René and Peggy Cusson.)

Camp Johnson, though it officially lies in the town of Colchester, sits very close to the Winooski border. Many Winooski men and women served in the US military, with the Vermont National Guard being a particularly popular branch for local residents. This photograph shows Company D, Maintenance, of the Winooski Armory. (Courtesy of René and Peggy Cusson.)

Eight

REVITALIZATION

Looking up the west side of Main Street, this photograph shows an area of the city untouched by the Model Cities Program. Although ownership has changed greatly in this area, many of the buildings have remained fundamentally the same. In other parts of Winooski, the Model Cities Program led to the demolition of entire blocks.

This image shows the east side of Main Street in the late 1950s, prior to the removal of these buildings under the Model Cities Program and before reconstruction in the mid-1970s. For many years, this was considered the heart of downtown Winooski.

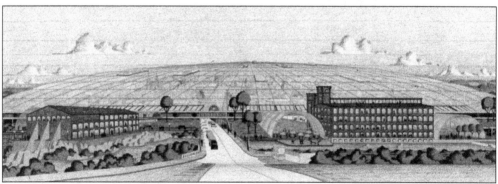

In 1979, Winooski's Community Development Committee applied for $55,000 in federal funding to study the feasibility of building a single dome over the city or two separate domes—one over the downtown area and the other over the industrial park. Proponents of the plan believed that the dome would significantly reduce heating costs within the city. They hoped, ideally, that it would be retractable for sunny days. In March 1980, a two-day symposium to review the plan was held at St. Michael's College. Buckminster Fuller, inventor of the geodesic dome, was the keynote speaker. Many spoke for and against the plans. In the end, a request for federal funding to study the option and to build the dome was denied.

As part of the Model Cities Program, Winooski's governmental officials applied for an Urban Renewal Grant. Citing eminent domain, officials confiscated the land east of Main Street, between East Allen Street and the Champlain Mill, and proceeded to demolish the buildings. Demolition of the buildings began in the early 1970s. These photographs, taken by Dan Higgins, show both Main and East Allen Streets in 1973. Although intended to revitalize the city, the Model Cities Program was widely considered a failure. Many historic buildings were destroyed, and a great deal of the promised new construction did not occur. (Courtesy of Dan Higgins.)

Winooski, as seen from the top of the Champlain Mill, is shown prior to the renaissance project. After construction, the parking lots—used for a series of stores, offices, and restaurants—would become a large parking garage with wraparound commercial spaces.

Site demolition included removing many of the trees that had been planted during the renaissance project of 1979. Photographer Dan Higgins, who documented both projects, described the project in *Vacancy, Art & Transformation* as follows: "Bulldozers easily demolished the commercial brick buildings that had made up the shopping mall. Then they tore up the asphalt parking lot and knocked down the small bank at the corner. From the Winooski Block it looked as though time had stood still. None of the construction of the 1980s had left any trace, disappearing much as the neighborhood thirty years before." (Courtesy of Alfred Blondin.)

Taken from the roof of the Champlain Mill in 2001 by Al Blondin, this photograph shows the parking lot and shopping complex that were removed to make way for new construction. The structures being removed were part of an earlier attempt to rebuild the area after the failure of the Model Cities Program. Kennett's IGA, Mahoney Hardware Store, Denny's Restaurant, and Higher Ground Night Club were demolished for the renaissance project. (Courtesy of Alfred Blondin.)

Created by the Dan Higgins Photo Studio, this fusion image shows the old east side of Winooski joined to the present-day Winooski via the traffic rotary. The image gives a sense of just how many changes have been made to the landscape of the city, first through Model Cities and various renovation projects and then through the renaissance project.

The Winooski Block, since the "big dig" of 2004 and 2005, now sits at the north end of a rotary circle. Designed to accommodate the demands of increasing automobile traffic in the city, the roundabout encircles a park. Businesses surround the traffic circle, which offers relatively easy pedestrian movement as well. (Courtesy of Alfred Blondin.)

With the financial viability of the businesses surrounding the Champlain Mill and Winooski Block declining by the late 1990s, change needed to come to the Onion City. A multimillion-dollar plan called for the construction of a high-rise office and retail space, along with a 900-car parking garage, a hotel, and 800 new housing units in the form of apartments or condominiums. (Courtesy of Alfred Blondin.)

Construction on the south side of East Allen Street began in the fall of 2004. A year later, contractors were erecting steel buildings, all of which were then covered with blue and yellow Styrofoam walls. Bricks were later added to harken back to an earlier time. (Courtesy of Alfred Blondin.)

As part of the renaissance project, a wraparound building was created. The ground floor of the structure houses commercial establishments, while the upper floors house local students from Champlain College and the University of Vermont. At the center—hidden from view—is a parking garage. The Winooski Block is visible in the back left. (Courtesy of Alfred Blondin.)

The west end of the wraparound building is shown here during its 2004 construction. Visible are the parking garage and traffic rotary, both still being built, and the Winooski Block (to the left). As with the other construction photographs, this image was taken by Al Blondin, from the roof of the Champlain Mill. (Courtesy of Alfred Blondin.)

This photograph, which shows construction from the renaissance project, also offers a view of the Vermont Student Assistance Corporation (VSAC) building. VSAC, a public nonprofit agency created in 1965 to assist Vermonters with post–high school education and training, has four floors of office space, which spread over an entire block. (Courtesy of Alfred Blondin.)

Nine

THE FLOOD OF 1927

A truly devastating force in Winooski, the flood of 1927 actually affected all of Vermont. In fact, some 1,285 bridges and unknown miles of roads and railroads were washed away during the flooding, which was caused by average rainfalls of four to nine inches over three days (November 2 to 4), after a very rainy October.

Here is the steel bridge that connected Winooski and Burlington just hours before the flood took it away on November 4, 1927. Virtually every family in Winooski at the time had a story about a member who was "the last" to walk across the bridge before the flood destroyed it.

When Herbert Hoover, the secretary of commerce, visited Vermont to view the damages wrought by the flood, he said that he was witnessing "Vermont at her worst, but Vermonters at their best." The General Assembly of the State of Vermont voted an $8.5 million bond issue in November 1927 and further assumed responsibility for highway maintenance in an effort to rebuild the state's infrastructure.

This image shows the Champlain Mill and Ready Block, both of which seem to be emerged in water, on November 4, 1927, moments after the bridge between Winooski and Burlington was swept away. This image was taken from the Burlington side of the river.

Eighty-four people, including Lt. Gov. S. Hollister Jackson, died during the 1927 flood, and 10,000 people were left homeless. Buildings like those of the Winooski mills were also destroyed by the flooding and required considerable work to clean and repair.

The east end of the Champlain Mill was torn apart during the flood of 1927. This portion of the structure contained the turbines that generated power for the mill's operations. Although the turbines were designed to harness the waters of the Winooski River, the flood proved too forceful for them.

This photograph offers a vision of Winooski, as seen from Burlington moments before the flood took out the steel bridge. The white building to the right is the Ready Block. The Champlain Mill is just out of sight to the right of the Ready Block.

Taken from the Winooski side of the river, this image shows Colchester Avenue. The three-story brick mill, which included 24 bays, also had a waterwheel. Originally the Burlington Mill Company (1892), the name of the factory changed when the Chace Mills of Fall River, Massachusetts, purchased the facility in 1912.

US Routes 2 and 7 ran through Winooski via the steel bridge that existed prior to the 1927 flood. Route 7 crosses the entire length of Vermont, allowing travel between the north and south. Although it has a less direct path, Route 2 allows travel from the easternmost and westernmost parts of the state.

The flood affected Vermont's political life as much as its social and economic life. After the flood, John E. Weeks became the first governor to serve two terms since the Vermont Constitution was amended to provide for a two-year term in 1870. Vermont also accepted more than $2.5 million from the federal government to help repair highways and bridges, another break in tradition.

In 1928, when Calvin Coolidge returned to Vermont, the state of his birth, he expressed the effect that the previous year's flood and the subsequent recovery efforts had on him: "It is gratifying to note the splendid recovery from the great catastrophe which overtook the state nearly a year ago. Transportation has been restored. The railroads are in a better condition than before. The highways are open to traffic for those who wish to travel by automobile."

Ten

BACK WHEN

Situated on Weaver Street, this house was home to Francis Le Clair, a local businessman and philanthropist. Besides his brickyard and the Winooski Block, Le Clair was noted for building and either selling or renting houses for low-to-moderate-income families. Additionally, Le Clair sold the lot now occupied by St. Francis Xavier Church to the parish at a greatly reduced price. (Courtesy of *Look Around Winooski, VT.*)

Prior to the advent of electric trolleys, horse-drawn trolleys were used to transport people around Burlington and surrounding areas. By 1922, the Burlington Traction Company had established 12 miles of trolley lines, connecting Winooski, Burlington, and Essex Junction. Another line, the Military Post Street Railway Company started on Upper Main Street in Winooski and ran two miles, ending at Fort Ethan Allen. (Courtesy of John Fisher.)

In 1890, Arthur B. LaVigne went into partnership with Henry Clement in an embalming business located in the Winooski Block. Clement sold furniture in the front half of the store, while the embalming process was carried out in the back. A few years later, the partnership was dissolved and Arthur B. LaVigne opened his own business—LaVigne Embalmers—at 16 East Allen Street. The business remained at this location until 1962, when it moved to its present location at 132 Main Street. Tom LaVigne entered the family business in 1979, later purchasing it in 1986. In 2014, after 35 years, Tom LaVigne sold the business.

Long before ambulances were affiliated with hospitals, fire departments, and rescue squads, funeral homes provided the service for local residents. In the case of the LaVigne Funeral Home, that service lasted until about 1966. Bob LaVigne was one of the first funeral directors to leave this service behind, saying that many of the emergency calls were to the scene of accidents and that, as an undertaker, he was ill prepared to handle the injured. Other funeral home directors quickly followed suit.

The Winooski City Clerk's Office has been housed in various buildings. The first location was the Baxter Block, after which the office was situated in a separate building attached to end of the Winooski Block, where McKee's Pub is now located. This photograph shows that second location. Currently, the Winooski City Clerk's Office is at 27 West Allen Street.

Henry Albon Bailey was the first mayor of Winooski. An attorney, Bailey drew up the charter for the new city in 1922. His law practice was originally located in the Winooski Block, though it later moved to the family store on East Allen Street.

With a payroll of a little more than $60,000 a week, the American Woolen Company was Winooski's largest employer in 1921. The mill's general superintendent, John O'Brien, was nicknamed "Mr. Winooski." He had started working at the mill in 1907, when he was 15, and was known for helping with any problem brought to his attention.

This photograph celebrates the raising of a flag by the American Woolen Mills on June 14, 1917 (for National Flag Day and in support of World War I). Taken by the Burlington photographer Louis McAllister, the image is one of a panoramic series that shows a crowd of hundreds of people listening to speeches and attending the festivities.

River Street, shown here in August 1967, runs parallel to the railroad tracks. Among the families who lived on this street from the 1940s through the 1960s were the Plantes, Benjamins, Belairs, Frenches, Savards, Metiviers, Tronos, Coutures, Lefebvres, Bouchers, Langlois, Rabideaus, Harrises, Carrolls, Pichés, Johnsons, Augustinos, and Soutieres. (Courtesy of René and Peggy Cusson.)

In 1973, downtown Winooski included a host of buildings on Main Street before the Model Cities Program began. Here, one sees the White Bargain Store, run by the Alpert family from 1899 until the 1960s; a storefront occupied by F.E. Allard's Clothing Store from 1915 to 1930 and later Gladstone's Shoe Store from 1945 to 1965; and on the corner, a storefront occupied successively by City Billiards, Kanorkian's Barber Shop, the First National Store, Robert Menotti's TV Sales and Service, and Whitehurst Pharmacy.

Among the businesses on Main and East Allen Streets were Bill's Diner, Epstein's Market, Louie the Gs, the American Restaurant, Granger's Barbershop, and the Whitehurst Pharmacy. Each of these institutions was forced to close during Winooski's urban renewal program in the 1970s.

122

Not just a commercial district, Main and East Allen Streets contained a residential area composed of several homes and apartment buildings. Many of those homes are visible in this photograph, which looks west toward the Winooski Block, in the distance and to the right.

River Street, located in the West Ward of Winooski, was established as a working-class neighborhood in the mid-19th century. Many of the small one-and-a-half and two-story houses were home to mill workers. At least 100 years later, in 1998, the street continued to boast a mix of small houses and apartment buildings. (Courtesy of Anastasia Pratt.)

The structures at 128, 124, and 116 East Allen Street (from left to right above) were torn down during the "big dig" in Winooski to make room on the Winooski campus for the Community College of Vermont (below).

" THE WINOOSKI BRIDGE ", TAKEN JUNE 1927 BY JOHN EPSTEIN

The bridge is another iconic piece of Winooski, connecting the city to Burlington and showcasing the mills that line the river. Now leading directly to the traffic roundabout in the center of downtown Winooski, this bridge serves thousands of commuters every day.

WINOOSKI-BURLINGTON HIGHWAY BRIDGE, REPLACING ONE TAKEN OUT BY 1927 FLOOD. THE LONGEST DECK PLATE GIRDER IN VERMONT.

COMPLIMENTS OF
WINOOSKI SAVINGS BANK, WINOOSKI, VT.

125

BIBLIOGRAPHY

American Woolen Company. *American Woolen Company Mills,* 1921.
Carlisle, Lillian Baker. *Look Around Colchester, Vermont.* Chittenden County Historical Society, 1972.
———. *Look Around Winooski, Vermont.* Chittenden County Historical Society, 1972.
Fibre and Fabric: A Record of American Textile Industries in Cotton and Woolen Trade. Volume 62. October 9, 1915.
Schaefer, Inge. *Colchester.* Charleston, SC: Arcadia Publishing, 2003.

ABOUT THE WINOOSKI HISTORICAL SOCIETY

The Winooski Historical Society was founded in 1975 with a mission to preserve and share the history of the City of Winooski. In addition to programs and preservation activities, the society has created a museum to showcase the city's past. Located in the Champlain Mill, the museum is open to visitors throughout the week. More information about the Winooski Historical Society may be found at https://winooskihistory.wordpress.com/.

Visit us at
arcadiapublishing.com

CPSIA information can be obtained
at www.ICGtesting.com
Printed in the USA
BVHW010643180720
584020BV00017B/212